RELIGIONS OF THE WORLD
A LOOK AT BUDDHISM

by Racquel Foran

BrightPoint Press

San Diego, CA

© 2024 BrightPoint Press
an imprint of ReferencePoint Press, Inc.
Printed in the United States

For more information, contact:
BrightPoint Press
PO Box 27779
San Diego, CA 92198
www.BrightPointPress.com

ALL RIGHTS RESERVED.

No part of this work covered by the copyright hereon may be reproduced or used in any form or by any means—graphic, electronic, or mechanical, including photocopying, recording, taping, web distribution, or information storage retrieval systems—without the written permission of the publisher.

Content Consultant: Sungha Yun, PhD, Assistant Professor of Asian Studies and Religion, St. Olaf College

---

LIBRARY OF CONGRESS CATALOGING-IN-PUBLICATION DATA

Name: Foran, Racquel, author.
Title: A Look at Buddhism / by Racquel Foran.
Description: San Diego, CA: BrightPoint Press, Inc., 2024 | Series: Religions of the World | Audience: Grade 6 to 12 | Includes bibliographical references and index.
Identifiers: ISBN: 9781678206727 (hardcover) | ISBN: 9781678206734 (eBook)
The complete Library of Congress record is available at www.loc.gov.

CONTENTS

AT A GLANCE	**4**
INTRODUCTION	**6**
PRACTICING BUDDHISM	
CHAPTER ONE	**12**
THE HISTORY OF BUDDHISM	
CHAPTER TWO	**24**
THE BELIEFS OF BUDDHISM	
CHAPTER THREE	**34**
THE STRUCTURE OF BUDDHISM	
CHAPTER FOUR	**44**
BUDDHISM AND DAILY LIFE	
Glossary	58
Source Notes	59
For Further Research	60
Index	62
Image Credits	63
About the Author	64

AT A GLANCE

- Buddhism is the fourth-most-practiced religion. It started between the 600s and 300s BCE.

- Siddhartha Gautama established Buddhism. He had lived a life of wealth. But then he saw how other people suffered. He searched for a way to end suffering. He is known as the Buddha.

- There are two main branches of Buddhism: Theravada and Mahayana.

- Dharma refers to the teachings of the Buddha. The dharma guides Buddhists.

- Meditation is an important part of Buddhism.

- Buddhists believe that living things are reborn many times.

- Monks are men who have dedicated themselves to Buddhism. Some live in monasteries.

- Buddhists can practice Buddhism anywhere.

- Monasteries, stupas, pagodas, and temples are four types of Buddhist structures.

- Wesak is an important festival for Buddhists. It celebrates the Buddha.

INTRODUCTION

PRACTICING BUDDHISM

When Issan wakes, he lies quietly in bed. He is still learning the ways of Buddhism. His teachers and studies have taught him that how he starts his day is important. Issan gives thanks for waking up. He breathes deeply. He sets his goals for the day. At school he will focus on his studies. He will do his homework. Buddhism has taught Issan that how he treats people is important. He reminds himself to be kind and patient with others.

Now Issan is ready to **meditate**. He has a small shrine in his bedroom. A statue of the Buddha sits on a high shelf. Placing the Buddha above all else shows respect

People can practice meditation anywhere they choose.

Being kind to others is an important part of Buddhism.

for him. Issan sits on the floor in front of the shrine. He calms his mind. He tries to create love and kindness by wishing everyone happiness. Issan promises not to harm others. He wants to spread goodwill.

After ten minutes of meditation, Issan is ready to start his day. He remembers the lesson of his teachers to be mindful all day. Being aware of his body, breath, feelings, and mind is an important part of practicing Buddhism.

Issan meditates again before going to sleep. He thinks about his actions during the day. He recognizes his mistakes. Issan decides to do better tomorrow. He also celebrates what he did well that day. He will try to keep doing good things in the future.

A LONG HISTORY

Buddhism started in India thousands of years ago. Now, it is the fourth-most-practiced religion in the world. In 2022, more than 500 million people practiced Buddhism. Most of them lived in Asia.

People who practice this religion do not believe in a god. They see life as a cycle. People believe in rebirth. They focus on reaching nirvana. This is an end to all

People of all ages practice Buddhism.

suffering. It is also an end to the cycle of rebirth. People can reach nirvana by becoming enlightened. Lama Jampa Thaye is a Buddhist meditation master. He says enlightenment "simply means waking up. Waking up to what is the true nature of the world, what is the true nature of the mind."[1]

1

THE HISTORY OF BUDDHISM

Buddhism began sometime between the late 600s and 300s BCE. Buddhist tradition says a prince named Siddhartha Gautama started it. He lived in what is now Nepal, near India. Gautama had everything he wanted. When he was 29 years old, he left his home and saw the world for the first time. He found out that people were suffering. They lived in **poverty**. They struggled with illnesses and death.

Gautama realized everyone went through a cycle of birth, aging, illness, and death. He was moved by what he saw. He let go of all his belongings. He started looking for the path to enlightenment.

People have made statues of the Buddha.

The Buddha became enlightened while meditating under the Bodhi tree. A descendant of that tree is at the Mahabodhi Temple in India.

Gautama traveled as a poor man. He found out that neither wealth nor **asceticism** led to enlightenment. He decided the best way to live was the Middle Way. This was a place between the two extremes. He spent a long time meditating. He came up with the Four Noble Truths. These became important teachings in Buddhism. Meditating allowed Gautama to achieve enlightenment.

Gautama became known as the Buddha. *Buddha* means "awakened or enlightened one." For many years, the Buddha traveled around northeastern India. He shared the Four Noble Truths with people. His teachings are called the dharma. He traveled for 45 years. Some experts believe he died in 483 BCE. But others think he died later than that.

The Buddha's last words were "Strive on with awareness."[2]

ESTABLISHING BUDDHISM

After the Buddha's death, some people believe his followers met with each other. They wanted to put together the Buddha's teachings. A second meeting took place about one hundred years after the Buddha died. At the time, some Buddhist **monks** lived in Vaisali. This was in northeastern India. These monks were more relaxed with the rules of Buddhism. Most monks at the meeting did not like this. So some of the

People may begin practicing Buddhism at a young age.

Vaisali monks split from the religion. This was the first major division of Buddhism.

In the 200s BCE, the Mauryan Empire was growing in northern India. Control of land was won through bloody battles. Ashoka was the third Mauryan emperor. He did not like war. He began to practice

Buddhism. He rejected violence. Ashoka wanted other people to follow Buddhism too. He sent monks to share the Buddha's teachings. Buddhism spread throughout India and beyond.

RISE AND FALL IN POPULARITY

Buddhism was first introduced to China by the 100s CE. Chinese and other Asian-language translations of Buddhist texts appeared around 200 CE. Buddhist monuments and **monasteries** were being built too. These structures were made with the support of local rulers.

Ashoka ruled the Mauryan Empire from around 265 to 238 BCE.

Buddhism spread farther into Asia. Starting in 372 CE, areas of Korea began making Buddhism the official religion. Korea introduced Buddhism to Japan. Prince Shotoku ruled Japan from 594 to 622 CE. He supported and spread Buddhism in his country.

India's Gupta Dynasty lasted from 320 to 600 CE. During this time, Buddhist educational centers were built. They were called Mahaviharas, or "great monasteries." People studied Buddhist texts there.

By the 500s CE, different branches of Buddhism had developed. The two main

BUDDHISM TODAY

Buddhism spread throughout Asia over many centuries. Today, different branches of the religion are more widespread in certain countries. The largest branch is Mahayana. Theravada is the second-largest branch.

branches still practiced today are Mahayana and Theravada. By the 1100s CE, Buddhism's popularity had decreased in India. It had been mostly replaced by Hinduism and Islam. However, Buddhism remained popular throughout Asia.

EXPANDING WEST

Beginning around the 1600s, Europeans started taking over some Asian countries. Europeans returned home from these places. They shared what they had learned about Buddhism.

In the 1800s, books were written about Buddhism. They introduced the religion to Western nations. Some Westerners began to follow Buddhism. Some of them went to Asia and joined Buddhist monasteries. They became monks. At the same time, more Asian immigrants came to North America. As a result, Buddhism spread in Canada and the United States.

SKINNY AND LAUGHING BUDDHA

Statues of Siddhartha Gautama show a thin Buddha. But there are also statues of a fat or laughing Buddha. This laughing Buddha was modeled after a Chinese monk named Budai. He is a symbol of happiness, contentment, and prosperity.

2

THE BELIEFS OF BUDDHISM

The Buddha's teachings are called the dharma. They guide Buddhists on how to live. Buddhists believe that through meditation and living as the Buddha suggests, they can free themselves from human suffering.

Buddhists believe in rebirth. Living creatures can be reborn as many things, including humans or animals. How Buddhists live determines whether their new form will be better or worse than their old one. Karma plays a role in this. Karma says good actions will cause good results.

Buddhists believe in different kinds of suffering. One type of suffering is emotional distress.

Buddhists, including monks, meditate in order to find inner peace and enlightenment.

People will have happy lives. People will be reborn in a higher form if they are good. But bad actions cause unhappiness. They will lead to rebirth in a lower form. Examples of higher forms include humans, demigods, and heavenly beings. Lower forms include animals and ghosts.

THE PHILOSOPHIES OF BUDDHISM

The main **philosophy** of Buddhism centers on the Four Noble Truths. The first truth teaches that suffering exists. The second is that suffering has a cause. The third truth is that suffering must end. And the fourth is that there is a path to end suffering.

The Four Noble Truths help people understand that there is suffering in the world. They also tell people they can change it. Thich Nhat Hanh is a Vietnamese monk. He said, "When another person makes you suffer, it is because he suffers deeply within himself, and his suffering is spilling over. He does not need punishment; he needs help."[3]

Buddhists want to end suffering. They follow the Eightfold Path to do this. It is a guide to enlightenment. There are eight parts to it. First, people must understand the Four Noble Truths. Second, they must get rid of attachments and hateful thoughts. Third, they must avoid lying or saying hurtful things. Fourth, people cannot harm others. Fifth, they should not work at jobs that might hurt other things, such as animals. Sixth, Buddhists must get rid of negative thoughts and keep positive ones. Seventh, they must be aware of the world around them as well as their bodies, thoughts, and feelings. The last part in the Eightfold Path is to achieve concentration.

THE DHARMA WHEEL

The dharma wheel is a Buddhist symbol. The round shape represents the perfection of the Buddha's teachings. The rim stands for meditative mindfulness and concentration. The center of the wheel represents moral discipline. The number of spokes on the wheel can vary. Eight is the most common. They represent the Eightfold Path.

Buddhists believe in samsara. This is the constant cycle of birth, death, and rebirth. It is considered a cycle of suffering. One Buddhist text says, "Long is the cycle of birth and death to the fool who does not know the true path."[4] Buddhists believe people are trapped in samsara until they achieve nirvana.

VAJRAYANA BUDDHISM

Some people say there is a third main branch of Buddhism. It is called Vajrayana. Vajrayana Buddhism is largely practiced in Tibet. It was formed by people who thought Mahayana Buddhism had too many rules. However, some people say Vajrayana is part of Mahayana Buddhism.

SCHOOLS OF THOUGHT

There are two main schools of thought in Buddhism. These are Theravada and Mahayana. Both follow the Four Noble Truths and the Eightfold Path. But they have different reasons for becoming enlightened.

Theravada Buddhists focus on becoming enlightened for themselves. They want to be free from samsara. Theravada Buddhists believe concentration and meditation are the best ways to become enlightened. Joining a monastery helps with this. People there can focus more on their religion. Monks spend a

There are many Buddhist monasteries today, such as the Shechen Monastery in Nepal.

lot of time meditating. Theravada Buddhists who reach enlightenment are called arhats.

Mahayana Buddhists want to become enlightened in order to help others on this path. In Mahayana Buddhism, people who have achieved enlightenment but choose to stay on Earth to teach others are called bodhisattvas. Mahayana Buddhists see these people as role models.

3
THE STRUCTURE OF BUDDHISM

Mahayana Buddhism is a name for a group of many Buddhist practices. For instance, Zen Buddhism and Pure Land Buddhism fall under Mahayana. Both of these branches have different traditions, rituals, and beliefs. They have allowed new texts and teachings. Cultures and other religions have also influenced their beliefs and practices. Because of these things, Mahayana Buddhism does not have a single formal structure. Each branch and each culture has its own practices.

Although different branches of Buddhism may have different rituals, all believe in the Buddha's teachings.

Buddhist monks choose to live simply.

Theravada Buddhism is organized around sangha. This is the monastic community of monks and nuns. Their role is to spread the Buddha's teachings. Laypeople are also important to this branch of Buddhism.

MONASTERIES AND MONKS

Buddhists made monasteries. They wanted to keep the Buddha's teachings alive. People who have devoted themselves completely to Buddhism live in monasteries. They believe this is the best way to reach enlightenment.

Monks are the male members of the monastery. To become a monk, a person must first train as a novice. A teacher watches over him. The novices spend years studying and practicing the Buddha's teachings. Eventually, a novice can become a monk.

The fourteenth Dalai Lama is a Buddhist monk. He is also the former head of Tibet. To become a Buddhist monk, he said there are three steps people must take. "The initial stage is to reduce attachment towards life. The second stage is the elimination of desire and attachment to this samsara.

Then in the third stage, self-cherishing is eliminated," he said.[5]

NUNS AND LAYPEOPLE

Nuns are also a part of Buddhism. But there are fewer nuns than monks. That's because there are more rules on how to become a nun. Women don't have as

THE DALAI LAMA

Tibetan Buddhists believe in a line of Dalai Lamas. The Dalai Lama is a spiritual figure. He practices and teaches Buddhism. People believe that when he dies, he comes back to teach the dharma. The fourteenth Dalai Lama was born in 1935. When he was two years old, he was recognized as the **reincarnation** of the thirteenth Dalai Lama. He began his Buddhist training at age six.

many opportunities to take on leadership roles in Buddhism. But people are trying to change that.

Laypeople are not part of the monastery. But monasteries need laypeople for support. Buddhist monks do not have traditional jobs. They also do not grow food. Laypeople give monks money, food, and medicine. Laypeople can live in monasteries for short periods of time.

BUDDHIST TEXTS

There is no single **authoritative** Buddhist text. The Buddha believed teachings

Laypeople give monks what they need. That way, the monks can continue studying and practicing Buddhism.

Both young and old people study Buddhist texts.

should not be blindly accepted. Buddhists should question the texts. They should look for their own meaning. There are many important texts in Buddhism. But they help guide Buddhists. They do not control them.

The Tipitaka may be the oldest Buddhist text. It has three parts. The *Sutta Pitaka* has speeches given by the Buddha and other important Buddhist leaders. The *Vinaya Pitaka* has guidelines for how monks and nuns should live. The *Abhidhamma Pitaka* has writings that look deeply at Buddhist ideas.

MONASTICISM

Monasticism is a system that monks live by. Members of a monastery dedicate their lives to religious study. Monasticism is central to most Buddhist branches, but not all. For instance, in Japan, the Jodo Shinshu rejects monasticism.

4

BUDDHISM AND DAILY LIFE

Buddhism plays a role in people's lives starting at birth. Buddhist parents visit a temple before and after their baby is born. They get blessings from the monks. Sometimes the monks will visit the home after a baby is born. They do a celebration worship. There are ceremonies and food.

When children get older, they visit Buddhist temples for dharma classes. Parents are encouraged to meditate in front of or with their children. Thubten Chodron is a Buddhist nun. She says, "It is very good for children to see their parents sit still and

Both Buddhists and tourists are welcome to visit the Kek Lok Si Temple in Malaysia.

be calm. That gives them the idea that maybe they too can do the same."[6]

Buddhism does not have rules for marriage or what a family should look like. Marriage is not a religious event. The Buddha said a family is a social unit. *Family* has a broad definition. It includes single-parent households. It also includes unrelated groups of people living together.

Buddhists believe in rebirth. The Buddha said not to fear death. People will often chant Buddhist texts about life and death to bring comfort to the dying. After death, the sangha performs a funeral service.

At some weddings, the bride and groom receive a blessing from a monk.

Family and friends might also have a memorial service at a home or temple. People offer food, flowers, and incense to the Buddha. During this time, Buddhist texts are chanted.

THE SIX DIRECTIONS

Buddhists may worship the six directions. They do this by doing their duties and showing respect. Parents are viewed as the east part of the six directions. Spouses are west. Teachers are south, and friends are north. Employers are below. Religious leaders are above.

There are guidelines for each relationship. Children should support their parents and continue family traditions. They should have good behavior. In return, parents should guide their children. They should make sure their kids are educated. They give them

Parents may share Buddhist teachings with their children.

advice on important things, like choosing a partner.

Students respect their teachers. Teachers should educate to the best of their abilities. They should be good role models. Spouses should honor and love each other. They should take care of both the home and children. Buddhists should be honest, helpful, and generous with friends and family. As an employer, a Buddhist gives her employees fair pay. She should treat them well. In return, employees should be loyal, honest, and hardworking for their employer. Finally, Buddhists should be respectful of all religious people.

TEMPLES AND WORSHIP

There are different kinds of Buddhist structures that people can visit. Besides monasteries, there are also stupas, pagodas, and temples. A stupa is a

The Shanti Stupa is in Leh, India. It was built in 1991 to honor the long history of Buddhism.

Buddhist monument. It has sacred **relics** of the Buddha. Stupas have a round base. It supports a large dome. People pay their respects at stupas. They walk around the outside in a clockwise direction.

When burned, incense has a pleasant smell. Some Buddhists burn it to cleanse the area or to help create a peaceful atmosphere.

Pagodas are towers. They have many floors. They were built to hold sacred texts and relics of the Buddha.

Temples are places of worship. Unlike monasteries, they do not have areas where people can live. Temples usually have large halls for chanting. Buddhists visit temples. They can learn more about the dharma. Visitors offer flowers and incense to the altar of the Buddha.

FESTIVALS AND CELEBRATIONS

There are many Buddhist celebrations and festivals. Different countries celebrate

Buddhist events at different times. Even the new year is celebrated on different days. In countries where Theravada is practiced, like Thailand and Sri Lanka, Buddhists often celebrate the new year in April. Countries like China and Japan, where Mahayana is practiced, sometimes celebrate the new year in January.

For Buddhists, the new year is a time for self-reflection. People visit a temple. They light candles. They wish for good luck in the new year. People meditate. They think about how they can improve in the coming year.

People in Luang Prabang, Laos, honor the Buddha during Wesak.

Many Buddhist festivals celebrate life events of the Buddha. Wesak (also spelled Vesak) is the most important Buddhist festival. It takes place on the full moon in May. During this time, Buddhists visit a temple or monastery. They offer gifts to the altar of the Buddha.

Buddhism has been practiced for thousands of years. Geshe Lhador is a Buddhist monk. He explains how Buddhism can be practiced in the modern day. "Since we are all so connected, we need to learn how to appreciate . . . diversity rather than be threatened by it, and through that appreciation, there will be richness and harmony," he said.[7]

Buddhism is a complex religion. It has spread around the world. It has broken off into different branches. But the goal of many Buddhists is enlightenment. By reaching enlightenment, people can leave the cycle of human suffering.

FESTIVAL OF THE SACRED TOOTH

Sri Lankan Buddhists celebrate the Festival of the Sacred Tooth. This often happens in July or August. It is a ten-day event. It includes dancers, jugglers, and decorated elephants. The festival honors the sacred relic tooth of the Buddha. The first parade to honor the relic took place in the 300s CE.

GLOSSARY

asceticism
denial of desires for a spiritual purpose

authoritative
trusted to be true and accurate

meditate
to sit quietly and focus one's mind

monasteries
buildings where monks live and practice their religion

monks
religious people in Buddhism who live under vows of poverty, chastity, and obedience

philosophy
the study of reality and existence

poverty
the state of being poor

reincarnation
the rebirth of the soul after death

relics
historical objects with religious importance

SOURCE NOTES

INTRODUCTION: PRACTICING BUDDHISM

1. Lama Jampa Thaye, "What Is Enlightenment in Buddhism?" *YouTube*, May 16, 2019. www.youtube.com.

CHAPTER ONE: THE HISTORY OF BUDDHISM

2. Quoted in "The Birth and Spread of Buddhism," *Ancient Civilizations*, n.d. www.ushistory.org.

CHAPTER TWO: THE BELIEFS OF BUDDHISM

3. Quoted in "Wise Words of Thich Nhat Hanh," *Awareness of Mind*, n.d. https://awarenessofmind.com.

4. Quoted in "Death and the Afterlife," *BBC*, n.d. www.bbc.co.uk.

CHAPTER THREE: THE STRUCTURE OF BUDDHISM

5. Quoted in "How to Become a Monk or a Nun—Preparing for Ordination," *FPMT*, n.d. https://fpmt.org.

CHAPTER FOUR: BUDDHISM AND DAILY LIFE

6. Thubten Chodron, "Practicing Buddhism in Daily Life," *Venerable Thubten Chodron*, September 9, 2013. https://thubtenchodron.org.

7. Quoted in Tsering Namgyal, "Ethical Mindfulness: An Interview with Tibetan Buddhist Monk and Scholar Geshe Lhador," *Buddhist Door Global*, March 12, 2020. www.buddhistdoor.net.

FOR FURTHER RESEARCH

BOOKS

Fleur Bradley, *My Life as a Buddhist.* Ann Arbor, MI: Cherry Lake
Publishing, 2022.

Candradasa, *Buddhism for Teens: 50 Mindfulness Activities, Meditations,
and Stories to Cultivate Calm and Awareness.* Oakland, CA:
Rockridge Press, 2022.

Racquel Foran, *A Look at Hinduism*. San Diego, CA: BrightPoint
Press, 2024.

INTERNET SOURCES

"Buddhism," *Britannica Kids*, n.d. https://kids.britannica.com.

"Encountering the Buddha," *National Museum of Asian Art*, n.d.
https://asia.si.edu.

"What Is Buddhism?" *BBC*, n.d. www.bbc.co.uk.

WEBSITES

Buddhism: Basic Beliefs
www.uri.org/kids/world-religions/buddhist-beliefs

This website provides information on the history and principles of Buddhism.

The Buddhist Society
www.thebuddhistsociety.org

The Buddhist Society website is home to an extensive selection of resources about Buddhism. The society was established to publish and share the principles of Buddhism.

Soka Gakkai International-USA (SGI-USA)
www.sgi-usa.org

SGI-USA is a US community of Buddhists committed to living out the teachings of the Buddha.

INDEX

blessings, 44
bodhisattvas, 33

Dalai Lama, 38–39
dharma, 15, 24, 39, 45, 53

Eightfold Path, 28–29, 31
enlightenment, 11, 13–15, 28, 31, 33, 37, 57

Festival of the Sacred Tooth, 57
Four Noble Truths, 15, 27–28, 31

Gupta Dynasty, 20

karma, 25

laypeople, 37, 40

Mahayana, 21, 22, 30–31, 33, 34–35, 54
Mauryan Empire, 17
meditate, 7, 9, 11, 15, 24, 29, 31, 33, 54
Middle Way, 14
monastery, 18, 20, 23, 31, 37–38, 40, 43, 50, 53, 56
monks, 16–18, 23, 28, 31, 37–40, 43, 44, 56

nirvana, 10–11, 30
nuns, 37, 39, 43, 45

pagodas, 50, 53
poverty, 13
Pure Land, 34

rebirth, 10–11, 25–26, 30, 46
relics, 51, 53, 57

samsara, 30–31, 38
sangha, 37, 46
shrine, 7, 9
six direction, 48
stupas, 50–51

temples, 44–45, 47, 50, 53–54, 56
Theravada, 21, 22, 31, 33, 37, 54

Vajrayana, 30

Wesak, 56

Zen Buddhism, 34

IMAGE CREDITS

Cover: © Mongkolchon Akesin/Shutterstock Images
5: © Diana Hirsch/iStockphoto
7: © KP Suwannasuk/Shutterstock Images
8: © Dmytro Zinkevych/Shutterstock Images
11: © Tom Wang/Shutterstock Images
13: © Gim42/iStockphoto
14: © Radiokukka/iStockphoto
17: © Tanaphong/iStockphoto
19: © Kushwaha Artist/Shutterstock Images
21: © Red Line Editorial
25: © Alexander Ford/iStockphoto
26: © Jacob Wackerhausen/iStockphoto
32: © Omer Serkan Bakir/iStockphoto
35: © Fred Froese/iStockphoto
36: © Burak Can Oztas/iStockphoto
41: © enviromantic/iStockphoto
42: © szefei/Shutterstock Images
45: © Mike Fuchslocher/Shutterstock Images
47: © Pongstorn Pixs/Shutterstock Images
49: © Ronnachai Palas/Shutterstock Images
51: © Daniel Prudek/Shutterstock Images
52: © Radiokukka/iStockphoto
55: © aluxum/iStockphoto

ABOUT THE AUTHOR

Racquel Foran is a freelance writer from Coquitlam, British Columbia, Canada. She has authored several nonfiction titles for school-aged readers covering diverse subjects, including organ transplants, robotics, autism, and more. When she is not writing, Foran enjoys tending to her Little Free Library, painting, and walking her dogs along the banks of the Coquitlam River.